Stalin and the Chinese Revolution

Problems of the Chinese Revolution

Stalin and the Chinese Revolution

By

Leon Trotsky

Aspekt Publishers

Stalin and the Chinese Revolution

© Leon Trotsky
© 2022 Uitgeverij ASPEKT / Aspekt Publishers
Amersfoortsestraat 27, 3769 AD Soesterberg, The Netherlands
info@uitgeverijaspekt.nl – http://www.uitgeverijaspekt.nl

Cover: Snegina Uzunova
Inside: Sjoerd van 't Slot

ISBN: 9789464620030
NUR: 680

All rights reserved. No reproduction copy or transmission of this publication may be made without written permission.

Facts and Documents

The Chinese revolution of 1925-27 remains the greatest event of modern history after the 1917 revolution in Russia. Over the problems of the Chinese revolution the basic currents of Communism come to clash. The present official leader of the Comintern, Stalin, has revealed his true stature in the events of the Chinese revolution. The basic documents pertaining to the Chinese revolution are dispersed, scattered, forgotten. Some are carefully concealed.

On these pages we want to reproduce the basic stages of the Chinese revolution in the light of articles and speeches by Stalin and his closest assistants, as well as decisions of the Comintern dictated by Stalin. For this purpose we use genuine texts from our archives. We especially present excerpts from the speech of Khitarov, a young Stalinist, at the 15th Congress of the Communist Party of the Soviet Union, which were concealed from the Party by Stalin. The readers will convince themselves of the tremendous significance of the testimony of Khitarov, a young Stalinist functionary-careerist, a participant in the Chinese events, and at the present time one of the leaders of the Young Communist International.

In order to make the facts and citations more comprehensible, we think it useful to remind the readers of the sequence of the most important events in the Chinese revolution.

- March 20th, 1926 – Chiang Kai-shek's first coup in Canton.
- Autumn 1926 – the Seventh Plenum of the ECCI, with the participation of a Chiang Kai-shek delegate from the Guomindang.
- April 13, 1927 – *coup d'état* by Chiang Kai-shek in Shanghai.
- The end of May 1927 – the counter-revolutionary coup of the "Left" Guomindang in Wuhan.
- The end of May 1927 – the Eighth Plenum of the ECCI proclaims it the duty of Communists to remain within the "Left" Guomindang.
- August 1927 – the Chinese Communist Party proclaims a course toward an uprising.
- December 1927 – the Canton insurrection.
- February 1928 – the Ninth Plenum of the ECCI proclaims for China the course towards armed insurrection and soviets.
- July 1928 – the Sixth Congress of the Comintern renounces the slogan of armed insurrection as a practical slogan.

The Bloc of Four Classes

Stalin's Chinese policy was based on a bloc of four classes. Here is how the Berlin organ of the Mensheviks appraised this policy:

> "On April 10 [1927], Martynov, in **Pravda**, most effectively and in a quite Menshevik manner, showed the correctness of the official position which insists on the necessity of retaining the bloc of four classes, on not hastening to overthrow the coalition government, in which the workers sit side by side with the big bourgeoisie, not to impose Ôsocialist tasks' upon it prematurely."

What did the policy of coalition with the bourgeoisie look like? Let us quote an excerpt from the official organ of the Executive Committee of the Comintern:

> "On January 5, 1927, the Canton government made public a new strike law in which the workers are prohibited from carrying weapons at demonstrations, from arresting merchants and industrialists, from confiscating their goods, and which establishes compulsory arbitration for a series of conflicts. This law contains a number of paragraphs protecting the interests of the workers But along with these paragraphs there are others, which limit the freedom to strike more than is required by the interests of defence during a revolutionary war."

In the rope placed around the workers by the bourgeoisie the threads ("paragraphs") favourable to the workers are traced. The shortcoming of the noose is that it is tightened more than is required "by the interests of defence" (of the Chinese bourgeoisie). This is written in the central organ of the Comintern. Who does the writing? Martynov. When does he write? On February 25, six weeks before the Shanghai bloodbath.

The Perspectives of the Revolution According to Stalin

How did Stalin evaluate the perspectives of the revolution led by his ally, Chiang Kai-shek? Here are the least scandalous parts of Stalin's declaration (the most scandalous parts of it were never made public):

> "The revolutionary armies in China [that is, the armies of Chiang Kai-shek] are the most important factor in the struggle of the Chinese workers and peasants for their liberation. For the advance of the Cantonese means a blow at imperialism, a blow at its agents in China, and freedom of assembly, freedom of press, freedom of organization for all the revolutionary elements in China in general and for the workers in particular." [3]

The army of Chiang Kai-shek is the army of workers and peasants. It bears freedom for the whole population, "for the workers in particular".

What is needed for the success of the revolution? Very little:

> "The student youth (the revolutionary youth), the working youth, the peasant youth – all these are a force that can advance the revolution with seven league boots, if it should be subordinated to the ideological and political influence of the Guomindang."

In this manner, the task of the Comintern consisted not of liberating the workers and peasants from the influence of the bourgeoisie but, on the contrary, of subordinating them to its influence. This was written in the days when Chiang Kai-shek, armed by Stalin, marched at the head of the workers and peasants subordinated to him, "with seven-league boots", towards. the Shanghai *coup d'état*.

Stalin and Chiang Kai-shek

After the Canton *coup d'état*, engineered by Chiang Kai-shek in March 1926, and which our press passed over in silence, when the Communists were reduced to the role of miserable appendices of the Guomindang and even signed an obligation not to criticize Sun-Yat-Sen-ism, Chiang Kai-shek – a remarkable detail indeed! – came forward to insist on the acceptance of the Guomindang into the Comintern: in preparing himself for the role of an executioner, he wanted to have the cover of world Communism and – he got it. The Guomindang, led by Chiang Kai-shek and Hu Hanmin, was accepted into the Comintern (as a "sympathizing" party). While engaged in the preparation of a decisive counter-revolutionary action in April 1927, Chiang Kai-shek at the same time took care to exchange portraits with Stalin. This strengthening of the ties of friendship was prepared by the journey of Bubnov, a member of the Central Committee and one of Stalin's agents, to Chiang Kai-shek. Another "detail": Bubnov's journey to Canton coincided with the March *coup d'état* of Chiang Kai-shek. What about Bubnov? He made the Chinese Communists submit and keep quiet.

After the Shanghai overturn, the bureaux of the Comintern, upon Stalin's order, attempted to deny that the executioner Chiang Kai-shek still remained a member of the Comintern. They had forgotten the vote at the Political Bureau, when everybody, against the vote of one (Trotsky), sanctioned the admission of the Guomindang into the Comintern with a consultative voice.

They had forgotten that at the Seventh Plenum of the ECCI, which condemned the Left Opposition, "comrade Shao Li-tse", a delegate from the Guomindang, participated. Among other things he said:

> "Comrade Chiang Kai-shek in his speech to the members of the Guomindang, declared that the Chinese revolution would be inconceivable if it could not correctly solve the agrarian, that is, the peasant question. What the Guomindang strives for is that there should not be created a bourgeois domination after the nationalist revolution in China, as happened in the West, as we see it now in all countries except the USSR We are all convinced, that under the leadership of the Communist Party and the Comintern, the Guomindang will fulfil its historic task."

This is how matters stood at the Seventh Plenum in the autumn of 1926. After the member of the Comintern, "comrade Chiang Kai-shek", who had promised to solve all the tasks under the leadership of the Comintern, solved only one: precisely the task of a bloody crushing of the revolution, the Eighth Plenum in May 1927 declared in the resolution on the Chinese question:

> "The ECCI states that the events fully justified the prognosis of the Seventh Plenum."

Justified, and right to the very end! If this is humour, it is at any rate not arbitrary. However, let us not forget that this humour is thickly coloured with Shanghai blood.

The Strategy of Lenin and the Strategy of Stalin

What tasks did Lenin set before the Comintern with regard to the backward countries?

> "It is necessary to carry on a determined struggle against the attempt to surround the bourgeois democratic liberation movements in the backward countries with a Communist cloak."

In carrying this out, the Guomindang, which had promised to establish in China "not a bourgeois régime", was admitted into the Comintern.

Lenin, it is understood, recognized the necessity of a temporary alliance with the bourgeois-democratic movement, but he understood by this, of course, not an alliance with the bourgeois parties, duping and betraying the petty-bourgeois revolutionary democracy (the peasants and the small city folk), but an alliance with the organizations and groupings of the masses themselves – against the national bourgeoisie. In what form, then, did Lenin visualize the alliance with the bourgeois democracy of the colonies? To these, too, he gives an answer in his thesis written for the Second Congress:

> "The Communist International should enter into a temporary alliance with the democratic bourgeoisie of the colonies and backward countries, but should not fuse with it and must unconditionally maintain the independent character of the proletarian movement – even in its embryonic form."

It seems that in executing the decisions of the Second Congress, the Communist Party was made to join the Guomindang and the Guomindang was admitted into the Comintern. All this summed up is called Leninism.

The Government of Chiang Kai-shek as a Living Refutation of the State

How the leaders of the Communist Party of the Soviet Union appraised the government of Chiang Kai-shek one year after the first Canton *coup d'état* (March 20, 1926) may be seen clearly from the public speeches of the members of the Party Political Bureau.

Here is how Kalinin spoke in March 1927, at the Moscow factory *Goshnak*:

> "All the classes of China, beginning with the proletariat and ending with the bourgeoisie, hate the militarists as the puppets of foreign capital; all the classes of China look upon the Canton government as the national government of the whole of China in the same way."

Another member of the Political Bureau, Rudzutak, spoke a few days later at a gathering of the street car workers. The **Pravda** report states:

> "Pausing further on the situation in China, comrade Rudzutak pointed out that the revolutionary government has behind it all the classes of China."

Voroshilov spoke in the same spirit more than once.

Truly in vain did Lenin clear the Marxian theory of the state from the petty-bourgeois garbage. The epigones succeeded in a short time in covering it with twice as much refuse.

As late as April 5, Stalin spoke in the Hall of the Columns in defence of the Communists remaining inside the party of Chiang Kai-shek, and what is more, he denied the danger of a betrayal by his ally: "Borodin is on guard!" The coup occurred exactly one week later.

How the Shanghai Coup Took Place

In this connection we have the exceptionally valuable testimony of a witness and participant, the Stalinist Khitarov, who arrived from China on the eve of the Fifteenth Congress and appeared there with his information. The most important points of his narrative have been deleted by Stalin from the Minutes with the consent of Khitarov himself: the truth cannot be made public if it so crushingly proves all the accusations the Opposition directed against Stalin. Let us give the floor to Khitarov:

> "The first bloody wound has been inflicted upon the Chinese revolution in Shanghai by the execution of the Shanghai workers on April 11-12.
>
> "I would like to speak in greater detail about this coup because I know that in our party little is known about it. In Shanghai there existed for a period of 21 days the so-called People's Government in which the Communists had a majority. We can therefore say that for 21 days Shanghai had a Communist government. This Communist government, however, showed complete inactivity in spite of the fact that the coup by Chiang Kai-shek was expected any day.
>
> "The Communist government, in the first place, did not begin to work for a long time under the excuse that, on the one hand, the bourgeois part of the government did not want to get to work, sabotaging it, and, on the other hand, because the Wuhan government did not approve of the composition of the

Shanghai government. Of the activity of this government three decrees are known, and one of them, by the way, speaks of the preparation of a triumphal reception to Chiang Kai-shek who was expected to arrive in Shanghai.

"In Shanghai, at this time, the relations between the army and the workers became acute. It is known, for instance, that the army [that is, Chiang Kai-shek's officers – L.T.] deliberately drove the workers into slaughter. The army for a period of several days stood at the gates of Shanghai and did not want to enter the city because they knew that the workers were battling against the Shantungese, and they wanted the workers to be bled in this struggle. They expected to enter later. Afterwards the army did enter Shanghai. But among these troops there was one division that sympathized with the workers – the First Division of the Canton army. The commander, Say-O, was in disfavour with Chiang Kai-shek, who knew about his sympathies for the mass movement, because this Say-O himself came from the ranks. He was at first the commander of a company and later commanded a division.

"Say-O came to the comrades in Shanghai and told them that there was a military coup in preparation, that Chiang Kai-shek had summoned him to headquarters, had given him an unusually cold reception and that he, Say-O, would not go there any longer – because he feared a trap. Chiang Kai-shek proposed to Say-O that he get out of the city with his division and to go to the front; and he, Say-O, proposed to the Central Committee of the Communist Party that they agree that he should not submit to Chiang Kai-shek's order. He was ready to remain in Shanghai and fight together with the Shanghai workers against the military overthrow that was in preparation. To all this, our responsible leaders of the Chinese Communist Party, Chen Duxiu included, declared that they knew about the coup being prepared, but that they did not want a premature conflict with Chiang Kai-shek. The First Division was let out of Shanghai, the city was occupied by the Second Division of Bai-Sung Gee and, two days later, the Shanghai workers were massacred."

Why was this truly stirring narrative left out of the Minutes (p.32)? Because it was not at all a question of the Chinese Communist Party but of the Political Bureau of the Soviet Union.

On May 24, 1927, Stalin spoke at the Plenum of the ECCI:

"The Opposition is dissatisfied because the Shanghai workers did not enter into a decisive battle against the imperialists and their myrmidons. But it does not understand that the revolution in China cannot develop at a fast tempo. It does not understand that one cannot take up a decisive struggle under unfavourable conditions. The Opposition does not understand that not to avoid a decisive struggle under unfavourable conditions (when it can be avoided), means to make easier the work of the enemies of the revolution ..."

This section of Stalin's speech is entitled: *The Mistakes of the Opposition*. In the Shanghai tragedy Stalin found mistakes ... by the Opposition. In reality the Opposition at that time did not yet know the concrete circumstances of the situation in Shanghai, that is, it did not know how much more favourable the situation still was for the workers in March and the beginning of April, in spite of all the mistakes and crimes of the leadership of the Comintern. Even from the deliberately concealed story of Khitarov it is clear that the situation could have been saved even at that time. The workers in Shanghai are in power. They are partly armed. There is all the possibility of arming them far more extensively. Chiang Kai-shek's army is unreliable. There are sections of it where even the commanding staff is on the side of the workers. But everything and everyone is paralysed at the top. We must not prepare for the decisive struggle against Chiang Kai-shek, but for a triumphal reception to him. Because Stalin gave his categorical instructions from Moscow: not only do not resist the ally, Chiang Kai-shek, but on the contrary, show your loyalty to him. How? Lie down on your back and play dead.

At the May Plenum of the ECCI, Stalin still defended on technical, tactical grounds this terrible surrender of positions without a struggle, which led to the crushing of the proletariat in the revolution. Half a year later, at the Fifteenth Congress of the CPSU, Stalin was already silent. The delegates at the Congress extended Khitarov's time so as to give him a chance to end his narrative which gripped even them. But Stalin found a simple way out of it by deleting Khitarov's narrative from the Minutes. We publish this truly historic document here for the first time.

Let us note in addition one interesting circumstance: While smearing up the course of events as much as possible and concealing the really guilty one, Khitarov singles out for responsibility Chen Duxiu whom the Stalinists had until then defended in every way against the Opposition, because he had merely carried out their instructions. But at that time it was already becoming clear that comrade Chen Duxiu would not agree to play the role of a silent scapegoat, that he wanted openly to analyse the reasons for this catastrophe. All the hounds of the Comintern were let loose upon him, not for mistakes fatal to the revolution but because he would not agree to deceive the workers and to be a cover for Stalin.

The Organizers of the "Infusion of Workers' and Peasants' Blood"

The leading organ of the Comintern wrote on March 18, 1927, about three weeks prior to the Shanghai overturn:

"The leadership of the Guomindang is at present ill with a lack of revolutionary workers' and peasants' blood. The Chinese Communist Party must aid in the infusion of this blood, and then the situation will radically change."

What an ominous play on words! The Guomindang is in "need of workers' and peasants' blood". The "aid" was rendered in the fullest measure: in April-May, Chiang Kai-shek and Wang Jingwei received a sufficient "infusion" of workers' and peasants' blood.

With regard to the Chiang Kai-shek chapter of Stalin's policy, the Eighth Plenum (May 1927) declared:

"The ECCI assumes that the tactic of the bloc with the national bourgeoisie in the already declining period of the revolution was absolutely correct. The Northern expedition alone [!] serves as historic justification for this tactic …"

And how it serves!

Here is Stalin all the way through. The Northern expedition, which incidentally proved to be an expedition against the proletariat, serves as a justification of his friendship with Chiang Kai-shek. The ECCI has done everything it could to make it impossible to draw the lessons of the bloodbath of the Chinese workers.

Stalin Repeats His Experiment with the "Left" Guomindang

Further on, the following remarkable point is left out of Khitarov's speech:

> "After the Shanghai *coup*, it has become clear to everyone that a new epoch is beginning in the Chinese revolution; that the bourgeoisie is retreating from the revolution. This was recognized and immediately so stated. But one thing was left out of sight in connection with this – that while the bourgeoisie was retreating from the revolution, the Wuhan government did not even think of leaving the bourgeoisie. Unfortunately, among the majority of our comrades, this was not understood; they had illusions with regard to the Wuhan government. They considered the Wuhan government almost an image, a prototype of the democratic dictatorship of the proletariat and peasantry." [The omission is on page 33.]
>
> "After the Wuhan *coup*, it became clear that the bourgeoisie is retreating ..."

This would be ridiculous if it were not so tragic. After Chiang Kai-shek slew the revolution in the face of the Workers disarmed by Stalin, the penetrating strategists finally "understood" that the bourgeoisie is "retreating". But having recognized that his friend Chiang Kai-shek was retreating, Stalin ordered the Chinese Communists to subordinate themselves to that same Wuhan government which, according to Khitarov's information at the Fifteenth Congress, "did not even think of leaving the bourgeoisie". Unfortunately "our comrades did not understand this". What comrades? Borodin, who clung to Stalin's telegraph wires? Khitarov does not mention any names. The Chinese revolution is dear to him, but his hide – is still dearer.

However, let us listen to Stalin:

> "Chiang Kai-shek's *coup d'état* means that there will now be two camps, two armies, two centres in the South: a revolutionary centre in Wuhan and a counter-revolutionary centre in Nanking."

Is it clear where the centre of the revolution is located? In Wuhan!

> "This means that the revolutionary Guomindang in Wuhan, leading a decisive struggle against militarism and imperialism, will in reality be transformed into an organ of the revolutionary democratic dictatorship of the proletariat and peasantry …"

Now we finally know what the democratic dictatorship of the proletariat and peasantry looks like!

> "From this it follows further [Stalin continues], that the policy of close collaboration of the lefts and the Communists inside the Guomindang acquires a particular force and a particular significance at the present stage. that without such a collaboration the victory of the revolution is impossible."

Without the collaboration of the counter-revolutionary bandits of the "Left" Guomindang, "the victory of the revolution is impossible"! That is how Stalin, step after step – in Canton, in Shanghai, in Hankow – assured the victory of the revolution.

Against the Opposition – For the Guomindang

How did the Comintern regard the "Left" Guomindang? The Eighth Plenum of the ECCI gave a clear answer to this question in its struggle against the Opposition.

"The ECCI rejects most determinedly the demand to leave the Guomindang ... The Guomindang in China is precisely that specific form of organization where the proletariat collaborates directly with the petty bourgeoisie and the peasantry."

In this manner the ECCI quite correctly saw in the Guomindang the realization of the Stalinist idea of the "two-class workers' and peasants' party".

The not unknown Rafes, who was at first a minister under Petlura and afterwards carried out Stalin's instructions in China, wrote in May 1927 in the theoretical organ of the Central Committee of the CPSU:

"Our Russian Opposition, as is known, also considers it necessary for the Communists to leave the Guomindang. A consistent defence of this viewpoint would lead the adherents of the policy to leave the Guomindang, to the famous formula proclaimed by comrade Trotsky in 1917: Ô Without a tsar, but a labour government!', which, for China, might have been changed in form: Ô Without the militarists, but a labour government!' We have no reason to listen to such consistent defenders of leaving the Guomindang."

The slogan of Stalin-Rafes was: "Without the workers, but with Chiang Kai-shek!" "Without the peasants, but with Wang Jingwei!" "Against the Opposition, but for the Guomindang!"

Stalin Again Disarms the Chinese Workers and Peasants

What was the policy of the leadership during the Wuhan period of the revolution? Let us listen to the Stalinist Khitarov on this question. Here is what we read in the Minutes of the Fifteenth Congress:

> "What was the policy of the CC of the Communist Party at this time, during this whole [Wuhan] period? The policy of the CC of the Communist Party was carried on under the slogan of *retreat* ...
>
> "Under the slogan of retreat – in the revolutionary period, at the moment of the highest tension of the revolutionary struggles – the Communist Party carries on its work, and under this slogan surrenders one position after another without a battle: To this surrender of positions belongs: the agreement to subordinate all the trade unions, all the peasant unions and other revolutionary organizations to the Guomindang; the rejection of independent action without the permission of the Central Committee of the Guomindang; the decision on the voluntary disarming of the workers' pickets in Hankow; the dissolution of the pioneer organizations in Wuhan; the actual crushing of all the peasant unions in the territory of the national government, etc."

Here is pictured quite frankly the policy of the Chinese Communist Party, the leadership of which actually helps the "national" bourgeoisie to crush the people's uprising and to annihilate the best fighters of the proletariat and the peasantry.

But the frankness here is treacherous: the above citation is printed in the Minutes after the omission cited above by the line of periods. Here is what the section concealed by Stalin says:

> "At the same time, some responsible comrades, Chinese and *non-Chinese*, invented the so-called theory of retreat. They declared: the reaction is advancing upon us from all sides. We must therefore immediately retreat in order to save the possibility of legal work, and if we retreat, we will save this possibility, but if we defend ourselves or attempt to advance, we will lose everything."

Precisely in those days (end of May 1927), when the Wuhan counter-revolution began to crush the workers and peasants, in the face of the Left Guomindang, Stalin declared at the Plenum of the ECCI (May 24, 1927):

> "The agrarian revolution is the basis and content of the bourgeois democratic revolution in China. *The Guomindang in Hankow and the Hankow government are the centre of the bourgeois-democratic revolutionary movement.*"

To a written question of a worker as to why no soviets were being formed in Wuhan, Stalin replied:

> "It is clear that whoever calls at present for the immediate creation of soviets of workers' deputies in

this [Wuhan] district, is attempting to jump [!] over the *Guomindang phase of the Chinese revolution,* and he risks putting the Chinese revolution in a most difficult position."

Precisely: In a "most difficult" position! On May 13, 1927, in a conversation with students, Stalin declared:

"Should soviets of workers' and peasants' deputies, in general, be created in China? Yes, they should, absolutely they should. They will have to be created *after the strengthening of the Wuhan revolutionary government*, after the unfolding of the agrarian revolution, in the transformation of the agrarian revolution, of the bourgeois-democratic revolution into the revolution of the proletariat."

In this manner, Stalin did not consider it permissible to strengthen the position of the workers and peasants through soviets, so long as the positions of the Wuhan government, of the counter-revolutionary bourgeoisie, were not strengthened.

Referring to the famous theses of Stalin which justified his Wuhan policy, the organ of the Russian Mensheviks wrote at that time:

"Very little can be said against the essence of the Ôline' traced there [in Stalin's theses]. As much as possible to remain in the Guomindang, and to cling to its left wing and to the Wuhan government to the last possible moment: Ôto avoid a decisive struggle under unfavourable conditions'; not to issue the slogan ÔAll power to the soviets' so as not to Ôgive new weapons into the hands of the enemies of the Chinese people for the struggle against the revolution, for creating new legends that it is not a national revolution that is taking place in China, but an artificial transplanting of Moscow sovietization' – what can actually be more sensible ...?"

On its part, the Eighth Plenum of the ECCI, which was in session at the end of May 1927, that is, at a time when the crushing of the workers' and peasants' organizations in Wuhan had already begun, adopted the following decision:

"The ECCI insistently calls the attention of the Chinese Communist Party to the necessity of taking all possible measures for the strengthening and development of all mass organizations of workers and peasants ... within all these organizations it is necessary to carry on an agitation *to enter the Guomindang*, transforming the latter into a mighty mass organization of the revolutionary petty-bourgeois democracy and the working class."

"To enter the Guomindang" meant to bring one's head voluntarily to the slaughter. The bloody lesson of Shanghai passed without leaving a trace. The Communists, as before, were being transformed into cattle herders for the party of the bourgeois executioners (the Guomindang), into suppliers of "workers' and peasants' blood" for Wang Jingwei and company.

The Stalinist Experiment with Ministerialism

In spite of the experience of the Russian Kerenskiad and the protests of the Left Opposition, Stalin wound up his Guomindang policy with an experiment in ministerialism: two Communists entered the bourgeois government in the capacity of ministers of labour and agriculture – the classic posts of hostages! – under the direct instructions of the Comintern: to paralyse the class struggle with the aim of retaining the united front. Such directives were constantly given from Moscow by telegraph until August 1927.

Let us hear how Khitarov depicted Communist "ministerialism" in practice before the audience of delegates at the Fifteenth Congress of the CPSU. "You know that there were two Communist ministers in the government," says Khitarov. The rest of this passage is deleted from the Minutes:

> "Afterwards, they [the Communist ministers] stopped coming around to the ministries altogether, failed to appear themselves and put in their places a hundred functionaries. During the activity of these ministers not a single law was promulgated which would ease the position of the workers and peasants. This reprehensible activity was wound up with a still more reprehensible, shameful end. These ministers declared that one of them was ill and the other wished to go abroad, etc., and therefore asked to be released. They did not resign with a political declaration in which they would have declared: You

are counter-revolutionists, you are traitors, you are betrayers – we will no longer go along with you. No. They declared that one was allegedly ill. In addition, *Tang Pingshan wrote that he could not cope with the magnitude of the peasant movement*, therefore he asked that his release be granted. Can a greater disgrace be imagined? A Communist minister declares that he cannot cope with the peasant movement. Then who can? It is clear, the military, and nobody else. This was an open legalization of the rigorous suppression of the peasant movement, undertaken by the Wuhan government."

This is what the participation of the Communists in the "democratic dictatorship" of the workers and peasants looked like. In December 1927, when Stalin's speeches and articles were still fresh in the minds of all, Khitarov's narrative could not be printed, even though the latter – young but precocious! – in looking after his own welfare, did not say a word about the Moscow leaders of Chinese ministerialism and even referred to Borodin only as "a certain non-Chinese comrade".

Tang Pingshan complained – Khitarov raged hypocritically – that he could not cope with the peasant movement. But Khitarov could not help knowing that this was just the task that Stalin set before Tang Pingshan. Tang Pingshan came to Moscow at the end of 1926 for instructions and reported to the Plenum of the ECCI how well he coped with the "Trotskyists", that is, with those Communists who wanted to leave the Guomindang in order to organize the workers and peasants. Stalin was sending Tang Pingshan telegraphic instructions to curb the peasant movement in order not to antagonize Chiang Kai-shek and the bourgeois military staff. At the same time, Stalin accused the Opposition of underestimating the peasantry.

The Eighth Plenum even adopted a special *Resolution on the Speeches of comrades Trotsky and Vuyovitch at the Plenary Session of the ECCI*. It read:

> "Comrade Trotsky ... demanded at the Plenary Session the immediate establishment of the dual power in the form of soviets and the immediate adoption of a course towards the overthrow of the Left Guomindang government. This apparently [!] ultra-left [!!] but in reality opportunist [!!!] demand is nothing but the repetition of the old Trotskyist position of jumping over the petty-bourgeois, peasant stage of the revolution."

We see here in all its nakedness the essence of the struggle against Trotskyism: the defence of the bourgeoisie against the revolution of the workers and peasants.

Leaders and Masses

All the organizations of the working class were utilized by the "leaders" in order to restrain, to curb, to paralyse the struggle of the revolutionary masses. Here is what Khitarov related:

> "The congress of the trade unions [in Wuhan] was postponed from day to day and when it was finally convened no attempt whatsoever was made to utilize it for the organization of resistance. On the contrary, on the last day of the congress, it was decided to stage a demonstration before the building of the National government with the object of expressing their sentiment of loyalty to the government. (**Lozovsky**: I scared them there with my speech.)"

Lozovsky was not ashamed at that moment to bring himself forward. "Scaring" the same Chinese trade unionists whom he had thrown into confusion, with bold phrases, Lozovsky succeeded on the spot, in China, in not seeing anything, not understanding anything, and not foreseeing anything. Returning from China, this "leader" wrote:

> "The proletariat has become the dominant force in the struggle for the national emancipation of China."

This was said about a proletariat whose head was being squeezed in the iron manacles of Chiang Kai-shek.

This is how the general secretary of the Red International of Labour Unions deceived the workers of the whole world. And after the crushing of the Chinese workers (with the aid of all sorts of "general secretaries"), Lozovsky derides the Chinese trade unionists: those "cowards" got scared, you see, by the intrepid speeches of the most intrepid Lozovsky. In this little episode lies the art of the present "leaders", their whole mechanism, the whole of their morals!

The might of the revolutionary movement of the masses of the people was truly incomparable. We have seen that in spite of three years of mistakes the situation could still have been saved in Shanghai by receiving Chiang Kai-shek not as a liberator but as a mortal foe. Moreover, even after the Shanghai *coup d'état* the Communists could still have strengthened themselves in the provinces. But they were ordered to submit themselves to the "Left" Guomindang. Khitarov gives a description of one of the most illuminating episodes of the second counter-revolution carried out by the Left Guomindang:

> "The *coup* in Wuhan occurred on May 21-22 The *coup* took place under simply unbelievable circumstances. In Changsha the army consisted of 1,700 soldiers, and the peasants made up a majority of the armed detachments gathered around Changsha to the number of 20,000. In spite of this, the military command succeeded in seizing power, in shooting all the active peasants, in dispersing all revolutionary organizations and in establishing its dictatorship only because of the cowardly, irresolute, conciliatory policy of the leaders in Changsha and Wuhan. When the

peasants learned of the *coup* in Changsha they began to prepare themselves, to gather around Changsha in order to undertake a march on it. This march was set for May 21. The peasants started to draw up their detachments in increasing numbers towards Changsha. It was clear that they would seize the city without great effort. But at this point a *letter arrived from the Central Committee of the Chinese Communist Party in which Chen Duxiu wrote that they should presumably avoid an open conflict and transfer the question to Wuhan.* On the basis of this letter, the District Committee dispatched to the peasant detachments an order to retreat, not to advance any further; but this order failed to reach two detachments. Two peasant detachments advanced on Wuhan and were there annihilated by the soldiers."

This is approximately how matters proceeded in the rest of the provinces. Under Borodin's guidance – "Borodin is on guard!" – the Chinese Communists carried out very punctiliously the instructions of Stalin: not to break with the Left Guomindang, the chosen leaders of the democratic revolution. The capitulation at Changsha took place on May 31, that is, a few days after the decisions of the Eighth Plenum of the ECCI and in full conformity with these decisions.

The leaders indeed did everything in order to destroy the cause of the masses!

In that same speech of his, Khitarov declares:

"I consider it my duty to declare that in spite of the fact that the Chinese Communist Party has for a long time committed unheard-of opportunist errors.

we do not, however, need to blame the Party masses for them To my deep conviction (I have seen many sections of the Comintern), there isn't another such section so devoted to the cause of Communism, so courageous in its fight for our cause as are the Chinese Communists. There are no other Communists as courageous as the Chinese comrades."

Undoubtedly, the revolutionary Chinese workers and peasants revealed exceptional self-sacrifice in the struggle. Together with the revolution, they were crushed by the opportunist leadership. Not the one that had its seat in Canton, Shanghai and Wuhan but the one that was commanding from Moscow. Such will be the verdict of history!

The Canton Uprising

On August 7, 1927, the special conference of the Chinese Communist Party condemned, according to previous instructions from Moscow, the opportunist policy of its leadership, that is, its whole past, and decided: to prepare for an armed insurrection. Stalin's special emissaries had the task of preparing an insurrection in Canton timed for the Fifteenth Congress of the Communist Party of the Soviet Union, in order to cover up the physical extermination of the Russian Opposition with the political triumph of the Stalinist tactic in China.

On the declining wave, while the depression still prevailed among the urban masses, the Canton "soviet" uprising was hurriedly organized, heroic in the conduct of the workers, criminal in the adventurism of the leadership. The news of the new crushing of the Canton proletariat arrived exactly at the moment of the Fifteenth Congress. In this manner, Stalin was smashing the Bolshevik-Leninists exactly at the moment when his ally of yesterday, Chiang Kai-shek, was crushing the Chinese Communists.

It was necessary to draw up new balance sheets, that is, once more to shift the responsibility on to the executors. On February 7, 1928, **Pravda** wrote:

> "The provincial armies fought undividedly against Red Canton and this proved to be the greatest and *oldest shortcoming of the Chinese Communist Party, precisely insufficient political work for the decomposition of the reactionary armies.*"

"The oldest shortcoming"! Does this mean that it was the task of the Chinese Communist Party to decompose the armies of the Guomindang? Since when?

On February 25, 1927, a month and a half prior to the crushing of Shanghai, the central organ of the Comintern wrote:

> "The Chinese Communist Party and the conscious Chinese workers must not *under any circumstances* pursue a tactic which would disorganize the revolutionary armies just because the influence of the bourgeoisie is to a certain degree strong there"

And here is what Stalin said – and repeated on every occasion – at the Plenum of the ECCI on May 24, 1927:

> "Not unarmed people stand against the armies of the old régime in China, but an armed people in the form of the revolutionary army. In China, an armed revolution is fighting against armed counter-revolution."

In the summer and autumn of 1927, the armies of the Guomindang were depicted as an armed people. But when these armies crushed the Canton insurrection, **Pravda** declared the "oldest shortcoming" of the Chinese Communists to be their inability to decompose the "reactionary armies", the very ones that were proclaimed "the revolutionary people" on the very eve of Canton.

Shameless mountebanks! Was anything like it ever seen among real revolutionists?

The Period of Putschism

The Ninth Plenum of the ECCI met in February 1928, less than two months after the Canton insurrection. How did it estimate the situation? Here are the exact words of its resolution:

> "The ECCI makes it the duty of all its sections to fight against the slanders of the Social Democrats and the Trotskyists who assert that the Chinese revolution has been liquidated."

What a treacherous and at the same time miserable subterfuge! Social Democracy considers in reality that the victory of Chiang Kai-shek is the *victory* of the national revolution (the confused Urbahns went astray on this very same position). The Left Opposition considers that the victory of Chiang Kai-shek is the *defeat* of the national revolution.

The Opposition never said and never could have said that the Chinese revolution *in general* is liquidated. What was liquidated, confused, deceived and crushed was "only" the second Chinese revolution (1925-27). That alone would be enough of an accomplishment for the gentlemen of the leadership!

We maintained, beginning with the autumn of 1927, that a period of ebb is ahead in China, of the retreat of the proletariat, the triumph of the counter-revolution. What was Stalin's position?

On February 7, 1928, **Pravda** wrote:

> "The Chinese Communist Party is heading towards an armed insurrection. The whole situation in China speaks for the fact that this is the correct course Experience proves that the Chinese Communist Party must concentrate all its efforts on the task of the day-to-day and widespread careful preparation of the armed insurrection."

The Ninth Plenum of the ECCI, with ambiguous bureaucratic reservations on putschism, approved this adventurist line. The object of these reservations is known: to create holes for the "leaders" to crawl into in the event of a new retreat.

The criminally light-minded resolution of the Ninth Plenum meant for China: new adventures, new skirmishes, breaking away from the masses, the loss of positions, the consuming of the best revolutionary elements in the fire of adventurism, the demoralization of the remnants of the Party. The whole period between the conference of the Chinese party on August 7, 1927, and the Sixth Congress of the Comintern on July 8, 1928, is permeated through and through with the theory and practice of putschism. This is how the Stalinist leadership was dealing with final blows to the Chinese revolution and the Communist Party.

Only at the Sixth Congress did the leadership of the Comintern recognize that:

> "The Canton uprising was objectively already a 'rear-guard battle' of the receding revolution."

"Objectively"! And subjectively? That is, in the consciousness of its initiators, the leaders? Such is the masked recognition of the adventurist character of the Canton insurrection. However that may be, one year after the Opposition, and what is more important, after a series of cruel defeats, the Comintern recognized that the second Chinese revolution had terminated together with the Wuhan period, and that it cannot be revived through adventurism. At the Sixth Congress the Chinese delegate, Chan Fi-Yun, reported:

> "The defeat of the Canton insurrection has delivered a still heavier blow to the Chinese proletariat. The first stage of the revolution was in this manner ended with a series of defeats. In the industrial centres, a depression is being felt in the labour movement."

Facts are stubborn things! This had to be recognized also by the Sixth Congress. The slogan of armed insurrection was eliminated. The only thing that remained was the name "second Chinese revolution" (1925-27), "the first stage" of which is separated from the future second stage by an undefined period. This was a terminological attempt to save at least a part of the prestige.

After the Sixth Congress

The delegate of the Chinese Communist Party, Duxiu, declared at the Sixteenth Congress of the CPSU:

> "Only Trotskyist renegades and Chinese Chen Duxiuists say that the Chinese national bourgeoisie has a perspective of independent development and stabilization."

Let us leave aside the abuse: these unfortunate people would never be in the Lux boarding house if they did not address their abuse to the Opposition. This is their only resource. Tang Pingshan thundered in exactly the same manner against the "Trotskyists" at the Seventh Plenum of the ECCI before he went over to the enemy. What is curious in its naked shamelessness is the attempt to father us, Left Oppositionists, with the idealization of the Chinese "national bourgeoisie" and its "independent development". Stalin's agents, as well as their leader, fulminate because the period after the Sixth Congress once more revealed their complete incapacity to understand the change in circumstances and the direction of its further development.

After the Canton defeat, at a time when the ECCI in February 1928 – was steering the coarse towards an armed insurrection, we declared in opposition to this:

> "The situation will now change in the exactly opposite direction; the working masses will temporarily retreat from politics; the Party will grow weak which does not exclude the continuation of peasant uprisings. The weakening of the war of the generals as

well as the weakening of the strikes and uprisings of the proletariat will inevitably lead in the meantime to some sort of an establishment of elementary processes of economic life in the country and consequently to somewhat of an even, though very weak, commercial and industrial rise. The latter will revive the strike struggles of the workers and permit the Communist Party, under the condition of correct tactics, once more to establish its contact and its influence in order that later, already on a higher plane, the insurrection of the workers may be interlocked with the peasant war. That is what our so-called 'liquidationism' consisted of."

But, apart from abuse, what did Duxiu say about China in the last two years? First of all, he stated, after the fact:

> "In Chinese industry and commerce a certain revival was to be marked in 1928."

And further:

> "In 1928, 400,000 workers went on strike, in 1929, the number of strikers had already reached 750,000. In the first half of 1930, the labour movement was still further fortified in the tempo of development."

It is understood that we must be very cautious with the figures of the Comintern, including Duxiu's. But regardless of the possible exaggeration of the figures, Duxiu's exposition bears out entirely our prognosis at the end 1927 and the beginning of 1928.

Unfortunately, the leadership of the ECCI and the Chinese Communist Party took their point of departure from the directly opposite prognosis. The slogan of armed insurrection was dropped only at the Sixth Congress, that is, in the middle of 1928. But aside from this purely negative decision the Party did not receive any new orientation. The possibility of economic revival was not taken into consideration by it. The strike movement went on to a considerable extent apart from it. Can one doubt for an instant that if the leadership of the Comintern had not occupied itself with stupid accusations of liquidationism against the Opposition and had understood the situation in time, as we did, the Chinese Communist Party would have been considerably stronger, primarily in the trade-union movement? Let us recall that during the highest ascent of the second revolution, in the first half of 1927, there were 2,800,000 workers organized in trade unions under the influence of the Communist Party. At the present time, there are, according to Duxiu, around 60,000. This in the whole of China!

And these miserable "leaders", who have worked their way into a hopeless corner, who have done terrific damage, speak about the "Trotskyist renegades" and think that by this slander they can make good the damage. Such is the school of Stalin! Such are its fruits!

The Soviets and the Class Character of the Revolution

What, according to Stalin, is the role of the soviets in the Chinese revolution? What place has been assigned to them in the alternation of its stages? With the rule of what class are they bound up?

During the Northern Expedition, as well as in the Wuhan period, we heard from Stalin that soviets can be created only *after* the completion of the bourgeois-democratic revolution, only on the *threshold* of the proletarian revolution. Precisely because of this the Political Bureau, following right behind Stalin, stubbornly rejected the slogan of soviets advanced by the Opposition:

> "The slogan of soviets means nothing but an immediate skipping over the stage of the bourgeois-democratic revolution and the organization of the power of the proletariat."

On May 24, after the Shanghai *coup d'état* and during the Wuhan *coup*, Stalin proved the incompatibility of soviets with bourgeois-democratic revolution in this manner:

> "But the workers will not stop at this if they have soviets of workers' deputies. They will say to the Communists – and they will be right: If we are the soviets, and the soviets are the organs of power, then can we not squeeze the bourgeoisie a little, and expropriate 'a little'? The Communists will be empty windbags

if they do not take the road of expropriation of the bourgeoisie with the existence of soviets of workers' and peasants' deputies. Is it possible to and should we take this road at present, at the present phase of the revolution? No, we should not."

And what will become of the Guomindang after passing over to the proletarian revolution? Stalin had it all figured out. In his discourse to the students on May 13, 1927 which we already quoted, Stalin replied:

"I think that in the period of the creation of soviets of workers' and peasants' deputies and the preparation for the Chinese October, the Chinese Communist Party will have to substitute for the present bloc inside the Guomindang the bloc outside the Guomindang."

Our great strategists foresaw everything – decidedly they foresaw everything, except the class struggle. Even in the matter of going over to the proletarian revolution Stalin solicitously supplied the Chinese Communist Party with an ally, with the same Guomindang. In order to carry out the socialist revolution, the Communists were only permitted to get out of the ranks of the Guomindang, but by no means to break the bloc with it. As is known, the alliance with the bourgeoisie was the best condition for the preparation of the "Chinese October". And all this was called Leninism

Be that as it may, in 1925-27 Stalin posed the question of soviets very categorically, connecting the formation of soviets with the immediate socialist expropriation of the bourgeoisie. It is true he needed this "radicalism" at that time not in defence of the expropriation of the bourgeoisie but on the contrary in defence of the bourgeoisie from expropriation. But the principled posing of the question was at any rate clear: *the soviets can be only and exclusively organs of the socialist revolution.* Such was the position of the Political Bureau of the CPSU, such was the position of the ECCI.

But at the end of 1927 an insurrection was carried out in Canton to which a soviet character was given. The Communists had the power. They decreed measures of a purely socialist character (nationalization of the land, banks, dwellings, industrial enterprises, etc.) It would seem we were confronted with a proletarian revolution. But no. At the end of February 1928, the Ninth Plenum of the ECCI drew up the balance of the Canton insurrection. And what was the result?

"The current year in the Chinese revolution is a period of bourgeois-democratic revolution, which has not been completed. The tendency towards jumping over the bourgeois-democratic stage of the revolution with the simultaneous appraisal of the revolution as a 'permanent' revolution is a mistake similar to the one made by Trotsky in 1905."

But ten months before that (April 1927) the Political Bureau declared that the very slogan of soviets (not Trotskyism, but the slogan of soviets!) means the inadmissible skipping of the bourgeois-democratic stage. But now, after a complete exhaustion of all the variations of the Guomindang, when it was necessary to sanction the slogan of soviets, we were told that only Trotskyists can connect this slogan with the proletarian dictatorship. This is how it was revealed that Stalin, during 1925-27, was a "Trotskyist", even though the other way around.

It is true that the program of the Comintern also made a decisive turn in this question. Among the most important tasks of the colonial countries, the program mentioned: "The establishment of a democratic dictatorship of the proletariat and peasantry based on the soviets." Truly miraculous! What was yesterday incompatible with the democratic revolution was today proclaimed to be its foundation base. One would seek in vain for any theoretical explanation of this complete somersault. Everything was done in a strictly administrative manner.

In what instance was Stalin wrong? When he declared the soviets incompatible with the democratic revolution or when he declared the soviets to be the basis of the democratic revolution? In both instances. Because Stalin does not understand the meaning of the democratic dictatorship, the meaning of the proletarian dictatorship, their mutual relationship, and what role the soviets play in connection with them.

He once more revealed it best, even though in a few words, at the Sixteenth Congress of the CPSU.

The Chinese Question at the Sixteenth Congress of the CPSU

In his ten-hour report Stalin, however anxious he was to do so, could not completely ignore the question of the Chinese revolution. He devoted to it exactly five phrases. And what phrases! Indeed, "a lot in a little", as the Latinists say (*multum in parvo*). Desiring to avoid all sharp corners, to refrain from risking generalizations and still more from concrete prognoses, Stalin in five phrases succeeded in making all the mistakes still left for him to make.

> "It would be ridiculous to think, [Stalin said] that this misconduct of the imperialists will pass for them unpunished. The Chinese workers and peasants have already replied to this by the creation of soviets and a Red army. It is said that a soviet government has already been created there. I think that if this is true then there is nothing surprising in it. There is no doubt that only soviets can save China from complete dismemberment and impoverishment."

"It would be ridiculous to think." Here is the basis for all the further conclusions. If the misconduct of the imperialists will inevitably provoke a reply in the form of soviets and a Red army, then how is it that imperialism still exists in the world?

"It is said that a soviet government has already been created there." What does it mean: "It is said"? Who says so? And what's most important, what does the Chinese Communist Party say about it? It is part of the Comintern and its representative spoke at the Congress. Does it mean that the "soviet government" was created in China without the Communist Party and without its knowledge? Then who is leading this government? Who are its members? What party holds power? Not only does Stalin fail to give a reply, but he does not even put the question.

> "I think that if this is true then there is nothing surprising in it." There is nothing surprising in the fact that in China a soviet government was created about which the Chinese Communist Party knows nothing and about whose political physiognomy the highest leader of the Chinese revolution can give us no information. Then what is there left in the world to be surprised at?

"There is no doubt that only soviets can save China from dismemberment and impoverishment." Which soviets? Up to now, we have seen all sorts of soviets: Tsereteli's soviets, Otto Bauer's and Scheidemann's, on the one hand, Bolshevik soviets on the other. Tsereteli's soviets could not save Russia from dismemberment and impoverishment. On the contrary, their whole policy went in the direction of transforming Russia into a colony of the Entente. Only the Bolsheviks transformed the soviets into a weapon for the liberation of the toiling masses. What kind of soviets are the Chinese? If the Chinese Communist Party can say nothing about them, then it means that it is not leading them. Then who is? Apart from the Communists, only accidental, intermediate elements, people of a "third party", in a word, fragments of the Guomindang of the second and third sort, can come to the head of the soviets and create a soviet government.

Only yesterday Stalin thought that "it would be ridiculous to think" of the creation of soviets in China prior to the completion of the democratic revolution. Now he seems to think – if his five phrases have any meaning at all – that in the democratic revolution the soviets can save the country even without the leadership of the Communists.

To speak of a soviet government without speaking of the dictatorship of the proletariat means to deceive the workers and to help the bourgeoisie deceive the peasants. But to speak of the dictatorship of the proletariat without speaking of the leading role of the Communist Party means once more to convert the dictatorship of the proletariat into a trap for the proletariat. The Chinese Communist Party, however, is now extremely weak. The number of its worker-members is limited to a few thousand. There are about fifty thousand workers in the Red trade unions. Under these conditions, to speak of the dictatorship of the proletariat as an *immediate* task is obviously unthinkable. On the other hand, in South China a broad peasant movement is unfolding itself in which partisan bands participate. The influence of the October revolution, in spite of the years of epigone leadership, is still so great in China that the peasants call their movement "soviet" and their partisan bands – "Red armies". This shows once more the depths of Stalin's philistinism in the period when, coming out against soviets, he said that we must not scare off the masses of the Chinese people by "artificial sovietization". Only Chiang Kai-shek could have been scared off by it, but not the workers, not the peasants, to whom, after 1917, the soviets had become symbols of emancipation. The Chinese peasants, it is understood, inject no few illusions into the slogan of soviets. It is pardonable in them. But is it pardonable in the leading *chvostists* who confine themselves to a cowardly and ambiguous generalization of the illusions of the Chinese peasantry, without explaining to the proletariat the real meaning of events?

"There is nothing surprising in it," says Stalin, if the Chinese peasants, without the participation of the industrial centres and without the leadership of the Communist Party, created a soviet government. But we say that the appearance of the soviet government under these circumstances is absolutely impossible. Not only the Bolsheviks but even the Tsereteli government or half-government of the soviets could make its appearance only on the basis of the cities. To think that the peasantry is capable of creating its soviet government *independently*, means to believe in miracles. It would be the same miracle to create a peasant Red army. The peasant partisans played a great revolutionary role in the Russian Revolution, but under the existence of centres of proletarian dictatorship and a centralized proletarian Red army. With the weakness of the Chinese labour movement at the present moment, and with the still greater weakness of the Communist Party, it is difficult to speak of a dictatorship of the proletariat as the *task of the day* in China. This is why Stalin, swimming in the wake of the peasant uprising, is compelled, in spite of all his earlier declarations, to link the peasant soviets and the peasant Red army with the bourgeois-democratic dictatorship. The leadership of this dictatorship, which is too heavy a task for the

Communist Party, is delivered to some other political party, to some sort of a revolutionary *x*. Being that Stalin hindered the Chinese workers and peasants from conducting their struggle for the dictatorship of the proletariat, then somebody must now help Stalin by taking in hand the soviet government as the organ of the bourgeois democratic dictatorship. As a motivation for this new perspective we are presented with five arguments in five phrases. Here they are:

1. "It would be ridiculous to think";
2. "it is said";
3. "if it is true";
4. "there is nothing surprising in it";
5. "there is no doubt".

Here it is, administrative argumentation in all its power and splendour!

We warn: the Chinese proletariat will again have to pay for this whole shameful concoction.

The Character of Stalin's "Mistakes"

There are mistakes and mistakes. In the various spheres of human thought, there can be very considerable mistakes which flow from the insufficient examination of the object, from insufficient factual data, from a too great complexity of the factors to be considered, etc. Among these we may consider, let us say, the mistakes of meteorologists in foretelling the weather, which are typical of a whole series of mistakes in the sphere of politics. However, the mistakes of a learned, quick-witted meteorologist are often more useful to science than the conjecture of an empiric, even though it is accidentally substantiated by facts. But what should we say of a learned geographer, of a leader of a polar expedition who would take as his point of departure that the earth rests on three whales? Yet the mistakes of Stalin are almost completely of this last category. Never rising to Marxism as a method, making use of one or the other "Marxian-like" formulas in a ritualistic manner, Stalin in his practical actions takes as his point of departure the crassest empirical prejudices. But such is the dialectic of the process: these prejudices became Stalin's main strength in the period of revolutionary decline. They were the ones that permitted him to play the role which subjectively he did not want. The cumbersome bureaucracy, separating itself from the revolutionary class that conquered power, seized upon Stalin's empiricism for his mercenariness, for his complete cynicism in the sphere of principles, in order to make him its leader and in order to create the legend of Stalin which is the holiday legend of the bureaucracy itself. This is the explanation of how and why the strong but absolutely mediocre person who occupied third and fourth roles in the years of the rise of the revolution proved called upon to play the leading role in the years of its ebb, in the years of the stabilization of the world bourgeoisie, the regeneration of Social Democracy, the weakening of the Comintern and the conservative degeneration of the broadest circles of the Soviet bureaucracy.

The French say about a man: His defects are his virtues. Of Stalin it can be said: his defects proved to be to his advantage. The gear teeth of the class struggle meshed into his theoretical limitedness, his political adaptability, his moral indiscriminateness, in a word, into his defects as a proletarian revolutionist, in order to make him a statesman of the period of the petty-bourgeois emancipation from October, from Marxism, from Bolshevism.

The Chinese revolution was an examination of the new role of Stalin – by the inverse method. Having conquered power in the USSR with the aid of the strata who have been breaking away from the international revolution and with the indirect but very real aid of the hostile classes, Stalin automatically became the leader of the Comintern and by that alone the leader of the Chinese revolution. The passive hero of the behind-the-scenes apparatus mechanism had to show his method and quality in the events of the great revolutionary flow. Within this lies the tragic paradox of Stalin's role in China. Having subordinated the Chinese workers to the bourgeoisie, put the brakes on the agrarian movement, supported the reactionary generals, disarmed the workers, prevented the appearance of soviets and liquidated those that did appear, Stalin carried out to the end that historic role which Tsereteli only attempted to carry out in Russia. The difference is that Tsereteli acted on the open arena, having arrayed against him the Bolsheviks – and he immediately and on the spot had to bear the responsibility for his attempt to betray to the bourgeoisie a fettered and duped working class. Stalin, however, acted in China primarily behind the scenes, defended by a powerful apparatus and draped in the banner of Bolshevism. Tsereteli supported himself on the repressions of the power of the Bolsheviks by the bourgeoisie. Stalin, however, himself applied these repressions against the Bolshevik-Leninists (Opposition). The repressions of the bourgeoisie were shattered by the rising wave. Stalin's repressions were fostered by the ebbing wave. This is why it was possible for Stalin to carry out the experiment with the purely Menshevik policy in the Chinese revolution to the end, that is, to the most tragic catastrophe.

But what about the present left paroxysm of the Stalinist policy? To see in this episode – and the left zigzag with all its significance will nevertheless go down into history as an episode – a contradiction to what has been said, can be done only by very near-sighted people who are foreign to an understanding of the dialectic of human consciousness in connection with the dialectic of the historic process. The decline of the revolution as well as its rise does not move along a straight line. The empirical leader of the down-sliding of the revolution – "You think that you are moving but you are being moved" (Goethe) – could not help at a certain moment but take fright at that abyss of social betrayal to the very edge of which he was pushed in 1925-27 by his own qualities, utilized by forces half-hostile and hostile to the proletariat. And since the degeneration of the apparatus is not an even process, since the revolutionary tendencies within the masses are strong, then for the turn to the left from the edge of the Thermidorian abyss there were sufficient points of support and reserve forces already at hand. The turn assumed a character of panicky jumps, precisely because this empiric foresaw nothing until he had reached the very brink of the precipice. The ideology of the jump to the left was prepared by the Left Opposition – it only remained to utilize its work in bits and fragments, as befits an empiric. But the acute paroxysm of leftism does not change the basic processes of the evolution of the bureaucracy, nor the nature of Stalin himself.

The absence in Stalin of theoretical preparation, of a broad outlook and creative imagination – those features without which there can be no independent work on a large scale – fully explains why Lenin, who valued Stalin as a practical assistant, nevertheless recommended that the Party remove him from the post of general secretary when it became clear that this post might assume independent significance. Lenin never saw in Stalin a political leader.

Left to himself, Stalin always and invariably took up an opportunistic position on all big questions. If Stalin had no important theoretical or political conflicts with Lenin, like Bukharin, Kamenev, Zinoviev and even Rykov, it is because Stalin never held on to his principal views and in all cases of serious disagreement simply kept quiet, retreated to one side and waited. But for all that, Lenin very often had practical organizational-moral conflicts with Stalin, frequently very sharp ones, precisely for those Stalinist defects which Lenin, so carefully in form but so mercilessly in essence, characterized in his "testament".

To all that has been said we must add the fact that Lenin worked hand in hand with a group of collaborators, each of whom brought into the work knowledge, personal initiative, distinct talent. Stalin is surrounded, particularly after the liquidation of the right wing group, by accomplished mediocrities, devoid of any international outlook and incapable of producing an independent opinion on a single question of the world labour movement.

In the meantime, the significance of the apparatus has grown immeasurably since Lenin's time. Stalin's leadership in the Chinese revolution is just the fruit of the combination of theoretical, political and national limitedness with huge apparatus power. Stalin has proved himself incapable of learning. His five phrases on China at the Sixteenth Congress are permeated through and through with that same organic opportunism which governed Stalin's policy at all the earlier stages of the struggle of the Chinese people. The undertaker of the second Chinese revolution is preparing before our very eyes to strangle the third Chinese revolution at its inception.

Notes

1. **Sotsialisticheski Vestnik**, no.8, April 23, 1927, p.4.

2. **Die Kommunistische Internationale**, March 1, 1927, no.9, p.408.

3. **On the Perspectives of the Chinese Revolution**, p.46.

4. **ibid.**, p.55.

5. **Minutes of the Enlarged Executive of the Communist International**, [German Edition], November 30, 1926, pages 403-4.

6. **Izvestia**, March 6, 1927.

7. **Pravda**, March 9, 1927.

8. Sixteenth session of the XV Congress of the CPSU, December 11, 1927.

9. **Problems of the Chinese Revolution**, pp.125-7.

10. **Proletarskaya Revolyutsiya**, p.54.

11. **Minutes** [German edition], page 71.

12. **Sotsialisticheski Vestnik**, no.9 [151], p.1.

13. **Workers' China**, p.6.

14. **Minutes**, p.34.

15. **Minutes**, p.36.

16. **Die Kommunistische Internationale**, February 25, 1927, p.19.

17. **Pravda**, July 27, 1928.

18. **Pravda**, July 17, 1928, No.164.

19. From the written *Reply of the Political Bureau* to the Opposition theses, April 1927.

20. *Political Report of the CC to the 16th Party Congress*, **Pravda**, June 29, 1930.